VIEWPOINTS AND PERSPECTIVES

VIEWPOINTS ON THE BATTLE OF GETTYSBURG

★ PART OF THE PERSPECTIVES LIBRARY ★

KRISTIN J. RUSSO

Published in the United States of America by Cherry Lake Publishing
Ann Arbor, Michigan
www.cherrylakepublishing.com

Reading Adviser: Marla Conn MS, Ed., Literacy specialist, Read-Ability, Inc.

Photo Credits: ©pictore/Getty Images, cover (left); ©Mathew Brady/Library of Congress/Wikimedia, cover (right); ©Edward Caledon Bruce/Wikimedia, cover (middle); ©pictore/Getty Images, 1 (left); ©Mathew Brady/Library of Congress/Wikimedia, 1 (right); ©Edward Caledon Bruce/Wikimedia, 1 (middle); ©pictore/Getty Images, 4; ©Tipton & Myers/Wikimedia, 7; ©Andrew_Howe/Getty Images, 8; ©Library of Congress/Wikimedia, 11; ©The Print Collector/Newscom, 12; ©Library of Congress/Wikimedia, 15; ©Donaldecoho/Wikimedia, 16; ©Edward Caledon Bruce/Wikimedia, 18; ©Kurz and Allison/Wikimedia, 19; ©Timothy H. O'Sullivan/Wikimedia, 21; ©JT Vintage/Glasshouse Images/Newscom, 22; ©New York Public Library/Wikimedia, 25; ©Library of Congress/Wikimedia, 29; ©akg-images/Newscom, 31; ©Mathew Brady/Library of Congress/Wikimedia, 32; ©Library of Congress/Wikimedia, 35; ©Boston Public Library/Wikimedia, 36; ©Library of Congress/Wikimedia, 39; ©Liszt Collection/Newscom, 42; ©Everett Collection/Newscom, 44; ©Historica Graphica Collection Heritage Images/Newscom, 45; ©George Sheldon/Shutterstock, 45

Copyright ©2019 by Cherry Lake Publishing
All rights reserved. No part of this book may be reproduced or utilized in
any form or by any means without written permission from the publisher.

Library of Congress Cataloging-in-Publication Data has been filed and is available at catalog.loc.gov

Cherry Lake Publishing would like to acknowledge the work of The Partnership for 21st Century Learning.
Please visit *www.p21.org* for more information.

Printed in the United States of America
Corporate Graphics

Table of Contents

In this book, you will read about the Battle of Gettysburg, which took place during the American Civil War. Each perspective is based on real things that happened to real people who experienced the battle. As you'll see, the same event can look different depending on one's point of view.

Chapter 1 4
Georgia McLellan: Resident of the Town of Gettysburg

Chapter 2 18
Robert E. Lee: General, Confederate Army

Chapter 3 32
General Abner Doubleday: Union Army

Timeline 44

Look, Look Again 46

Glossary 47

Learn More 47

Index 48

About the Author 48

GEORGIA MCLELLAN
Resident of the Town of Gettysburg

Gin was my sister's nickname, not Jennie, as the newspapers reported. They got that wrong. Her full name was Mary Virginia—Gin or Ginnie for short. Some of the newspapers got much of the story wrong. They reported things that were completely untrue. If she were still here, she would set the record straight. That is the kind of person she was.

I wish you had had the chance to meet my sister. You would have liked her very much. She was a fiery, **feisty** person. She never backed down. She was a person you would want on your side of a fight, no doubt. Oh! How I needed her that day! My little boy was only 5 days old, and she and Mother had come to be with me to take care of me and my new little son. Ginnie was tireless, despite the unbearable July heat. When she was not caring for me or for the baby, she was baking biscuits for the **Union** soldiers.

Naturally, we support the Union soldiers. Ginnie was Union to the core. I think it stems from the early breakup of our own family. My father was a talented tailor, but he was unwell. Ultimately his illness led him to the poorhouse, and we were left to **fend** for

> **SECOND SOURCE**
>
> Find another source on this battle from a civilian's point of view and compare the information there to the information in this source. How are they different? How are they similar?

> **THINK ABOUT IT**
> Determine the main point of this chapter. Pick out two pieces of evidence that support that point.

ourselves. Ginnie and my mother took up work as seamstresses, and my sister, in particular, always made sure our family's needs were met, even as young as she was. I think the breakup of our family led her to believe strongly that a thing that belongs together should stay together. The nation is like a family, and it should remain one, a solid union.

I believe she was also pining to hear from her special friend, Johnston "Jack" Skelly, who was a Union corporal. Ginnie baked and cared for the Union soldiers in our midst during the horrible battle hoping that somewhere, wherever Jack was, someone was caring just as tenderly for him. Jack had given Ginnie his picture, and I think they may have had an "understanding," though she never told me for sure if they were engaged to be married. Now I will never know. No one will. The secret rests with Ginnie and with Jack, who has also died of war injuries.

Though Jack's death is heartbreaking, it is to be expected. He was a soldier. My sister was no soldier, but she was a fighter, and her death is a shock to us all. Ginnie had escaped death once, and perhaps that is

THE THEOLOGICAL SEMINARY, LOCATED IN THE WESTERN SECTION OF GETTYSBURG, WAS USED AS A HOSPITAL BOTH DURING AND AFTER THE FAMOUS BATTLE.

In 1861, 10 roads led to the town of Gettysburg. The number of easy access roads is among the main reasons the bloody battle took place in Gettysburg.

what made her feel **invincible**. My home's location makes it the perfect target for errant bullets and **artillery** shells. One shell even crashed through the roof! My sister fainted with fright, but once she recovered, she did not take cover in the cellar as the rest of us did. She stayed upstairs and continued her

TURNING POINT OF THE WAR

The Battle of Gettysburg was the turning point of the American Civil War. Before it, the **Confederates** were at an advantage, having won some key battles. But about one-third of the Confederate soldiers who fought at Gettysburg died. After the battle, the Confederate army was weakened and no longer the threat it had once been.

work in the kitchen. I told you my sister was brave. But now I am beginning to wonder if she were not also a bit foolhardy. The danger was very real. That was obvious to us all from the very first day of fighting.

When the battle broke out on July 1, 1863, we took cover in the cellar for the most part. But later in the day, when the gunfire slowed and it appeared that the Union soldiers had retreated to the hills, Ginnie left the house and brought food and water to the soldiers. This put her directly in the line of fire! She acted like this did not bother her at all. She had Isaac with her, a young boy who lives with us. It is just her way that she would pretend to be brave so as not to scare him. In any event, Isaac reported that our sister remained calm and got the job done. I am so proud of her.

On the second day of fighting, bullets buzzed constantly right by our home. They broke our

ON THE FIRST DAY OF FIGHTING, 50,000 SOLDIERS WERE ENGAGED IN BATTLE. THAT NUMBER DOUBLED THE SECOND DAY.

windows and shattered the brick on the outside of the house. When the artillery shell blew a hole in the roof, we left it upstairs in the attic where it fell. Luckily it did not explode. And though that event clearly frightened the invincible Ginnie Wade, she did not

By the second day of fighting, about 20,000 soldiers on both sides were killed, wounded, captured, or missing.

stop the work at hand. She continued to care for me and my baby son, and she continued to bake bread, which she handed out to nearby Union soldiers.

It was the third day of fighting, on July 3, 1863, when Ginnie lost her life. That morning, Ginnie and Isaac left the house to collect firewood so that Ginnie could continue baking bread. When she returned to the house, she ate breakfast and read from the Book of Psalms, which she often did for spiritual strength. Little did my pious and courageous sister know how soon her life would come to an end.

At about 8:30 in the morning, a Confederate bullet entered the house and lodged in the bedpost of the bed where I lay with the baby. Soon after, another bullet hit, penetrating two closed doors. Ginnie was standing, kneading dough for more biscuits, when the bullet hit her in the back and pierced her heart. She was only 20 years old.

I screamed with **grief** and fright, and my **pathetic**

cries were heard by nearby Union soldiers. They entered our house and led us all down to safety in the cellar through a hole made by an unexploded shell. They feared that if we stayed upstairs, we would be vulnerable to Rebel sharpshooters. My darling sister was wrapped in a quilt and buried temporarily in our backyard. Later, she was moved to a cemetery where she was laid to rest near Jack Skelly. He died 9 days after my sister from injuries he sustained in battle in Virginia. Ginny never even knew that he had been hurt.

    The newspapermen swarmed around us, eager to tell my sister's story. Somehow, they got her name wrong. As I said, her name was not Jennie as reported, though I feel like that is how she will forever be known. Some reporters looked for a sensational side to her story. Some made note of my father's illness and his unfortunate brushes with the law. They pointed out that my name is Georgia and Ginnie's name was

KNOWN AS THE THE GETTYSBURG GUN, THE CANNON LAST FIRED AT THE BATTLE OF GETTYSBURG NOW SITS IN THE FOYER OF THE RHODE ISLAND STATE HOUSE.

Virginia, and they implied that we were secret southern sympathizers. Naturally, this is untrue.

In fact, on the fourth day, as the Union Army claimed victory and the Confederate Army began its

After her sister Ginnie Wade's death, Georgia McClellan moved to Iowa. With help from the Women's Relief Corps of Iowa, a statue was erected in the cemetery where Ginnie is buried.

retreat, my mother climbed out of the cellar. She went to the kitchen and continued baking bread to give to the hungry and embattled Union soldiers. Now I see where Ginnie got her strength and courage—from our own mother, of course. We Wade women are strong women, and we will carry on Ginnie's work.

Of the more than 7,600 people killed at the Battle of Gettysburg, Ginnie was the only civilian killed during battle directly by gunfire. Though to me she will always be special, this is not a distinction I would have wished for her.

2

Robert E. Lee
General, Confederate Army

It is time to invade the North. This is our only option for securing a quick and decisive victory. Ending this war is my goal. Ending it with a victory is my duty.

Our men's **morale** is at an all-time high following our almighty success at Chancellorsville in May. The Army of the Potomac never stood a chance against our zeal. And their commander? Joseph

Hooker? There is not much I can say about his incompetence that has not already been said. Even President Abraham Lincoln recognizes it, and it is likely the reason he replaced Hooker with Major General George Gordon Meade.

FAMOUS CONFEDERATE GENERAL THOMAS JONATHAN "STONEWALL" JACKSON WAS MORTALLY WOUNDED BY HIS OWN MEN BY MISTAKE ON THE SECOND DAY OF FIGHTING IN THE BATTLE OF CHANCELLORSVILLE.

But I have no doubt I can beat Meade as well. Both Hooker and Meade attended the United States Military Academy at West Point, as I did. In a different time, long ago, perhaps we could have been friends. All I need to know now is that we learned the art of war at the same academy, and I can guess their strategies and know their minds. I can win the battles that will lead to victory in war. But I must make my move now. I must capture this energy, this enthusiasm for victory among my men, before we lose it.

Another benefit I hope will come from a victory in the North will be recognition from potential **allies** in Europe. Without official recognition as a nation from Britain and France, we face challenges asking for legitimacy from other sovereign nations. Once Britain and France see that the North is a losing cause, they will join our side, and we will have the international support we will need once this war ends. This could be the decisive battle that brings all of our suffering to a close.

But first, of course, we must win.

I know that Meade has ordered his Army of the Potomac to pursue us into Maryland and southern Pennsylvania, but we are 75,000 troops strong. Meade's army is hardly a threat to us. My challenge will be to bring the fighting back to the North. Now that we are in southern Pennsylvania, surely Meade will follow.

MEADE TOOK OVER THE FARMHOUSE AND BARN OF WIDOW LYDIA LEISTER AND HER SIX CHILDREN AS HIS HEADQUARTERS DURING THE BATTLE.

More general officers were killed at Gettysburg than at any other battle during the Civil War. Nine were killed or seriously wounded.

Ha! It's just as I thought. Meade's army is on its way. I have issued orders for all regiments to assemble here in southern Pennsylvania. My headquarters is in a place called Cashtown. We have filled the place with 60,000 of our troops. They are itching to fight.

What is more, I have faith in all my generals. I do not believe the same can be said for President Lincoln. I have Jubal Early, whom I affectionately call "Bad Old Man," because he is such a curmudgeon. He inspires his men, though, and they call him "Old Jubilee." He is much loved and respected. And of course I have James Longstreet. I personally would follow him anywhere and know his men feel the same. And I know that neither Richard Ewell nor George Pickett will let me down. They are experienced and skilled army men. I am surrounded by knowledgeable and brave men, as a solid leader should be. Together, we will craft a victory in the North and bring this war to a close.

It is July 1, 1863, day one of the Gettysburg

ANALYZE THIS

Analyze the opinions and motivation behind the war in the first and second chapters. How are the perspectives different? How are they the same?

campaign. I have sent General Henry Heth on ahead. He will lead us to Gettysburg, a small farming town about 7 miles (11 kilometers) north of Cashtown. I hope the sheer size of our army will result in a quick northern surrender. They have not won a major battle yet. And, with Chancellorsville so fresh on everyone's mind, how can they think that they will be successful here?

There has been a **setback** already, but it is a small one and one we can certainly overcome. One of the divisions under General Ambrose Powell Hill reports that they arrived in what they hoped would be an unprotected town, but they found that Union troops had arrived first. Two Union cavalry brigades had to be pushed back a half a mile south to Cemetery Hill, but Hill and Ewell agreed that this was easily done, as

GENERAL ROBERT E. LEE TOOK OVER 70-YEAR-OLD WIDOW MARY THOMPSON'S HOUSE FOR HIS HEADQUARTERS DURING THE FIGHTING.

the Union troops were outnumbered.

This tells me that I must take advantage of our superiority in northern territory while we have it. Delaying an attack will only allow time for more Union troops to arrive. I have given discretionary orders for Hill and Ewell to attack the divisions that have sought refuge on Cemetery Hill. This means they can attack or not attack. The decision is at their discretion. I trust their judgment.

Unfortunately, in hindsight, I believe I should have issued straight orders rather than discretionary orders to attack. Neither Ewell nor Hill acted in a timely manner. By sundown, another Union corps arrived and strengthened the Union troops along Cemetery Ridge. And overnight, three more Union corps arrived and have now occupied Cemetery Ridge all the way up to a hill known as Little Round Top. Despite these setbacks, I must believe victory is within our reach.

By day two of this campaign, it is becoming harder and harder to believe in an easy victory. The Union Army has now occupied Culp's Hill to Cemetery Ridge. Longstreet advises a defensive maneuver, now that he sees the strength of the Union's position. I do not agree with this. I feel that if there was ever a time for outright aggression, that time is now!

I have ordered Longstreet to lead an attack on Union troops from the left, and I have sent Ewell to lead a strike from the right, near Culp's Hill. I issued this order and meant for it to take place as early in the morning as possible. I am frustrated beyond measure that Longstreet did not act on my order until 4 o'clock in the afternoon.

Once Longstreet's corps opened fire, the battle was brutal and bloody. I wonder if such violence could have been avoided if Longstreet had not waited for the Union soldiers to prepare. The only thing hindsight will help me with now, however, is to wonder how trustworthy my second-in-command, Longstreet, actually is.

For hours, our men fought with courage and valor. As the battle raged on, the Union troops made their way over a pile of boulders—known as Devil's Den—into a peach orchard. They also took a wheat field near Little Round Top. While the Union soldiers were able to hold Little Round Top, we beat them soundly at Devil's Den and in the peach orchard.

At the end of day two, reports are that there are more than 9,000 casualties on both the Union and the Confederate sides. This is certainly not the easy victory that I had hoped for, and even expected, but we must continue the fight. We have no choice. This is our moment, and if we lose it, this horrific war could

NUMBER OF CASUALTIES

Nearly 160,000 soldiers fought at the Battle of Gettysburg. About 51,000 men were killed or wounded in the battle. It was the bloodiest battle of the American Civil War. More than one-third of General Lee's troops that fought at Gettysburg were killed or wounded. The South was unable to recover from these heavy losses.

GENERAL PICKETT SOUGHT PERMISSION TO BEGIN THE ATTACK. THIS BECAME KNOWN AS PICKETT'S CHARGE.

SECOND SOURCE

Find another source telling the story of Gettysburg from a Confederate soldier's point of view. Compare the information there to the information in this source.

drag on endlessly.

On day three of the Gettysburg campaign, I am determined to settle this matter once and for all. I will call on George Pickett to put an end to Union aggression here. I have ordered him to lead a division of about 15,000 troops up and across about a three-quarter mile stretch to where the Union troops have dug in. Longstreet protests vehemently, but my trust in him has wavered. I will rely on Pickett to lead us to success.

As ordered, Pickett's charge set off at about 3 o'clock in the afternoon. An artillery bombardment was meant to weaken the Union target, but Pickett's men still faced the challenge of running uphill toward their opponents. I believe I made a grave misjudgment here. Union troops had been reinforced once again

BETWEEN 12,500 AND 15,000 CONFEDERATE SOLDIERS TOOK PART IN THE ASSAULT AND SUFFERED HEAVY LOSSES.

with regiments from Vermont, New York, and Ohio. Pickett's men were no match for the artillery volley, and Pickett lost two-thirds of the men in his division. As general, I know the fault is all mine. This is a bloody loss, but at long last, the campaign is over.

I have commanded my regiments to retreat. On day four, July 4, 1863, our troops began the retreat toward Virginia. I have to believe that one day we will be victorious on Union soil, but today is not that day.

GENERAL ABNER DOUBLEDAY

Union Army

General John F. Reynolds has been killed!

I must tell you, I am in absolute shock. Reynolds was my immediate superior—a good man and a good friend. Amazingly, I have been assigned to replace him.

Oh! What a sad loss so early in this campaign. Reynolds was shot and killed during a small, early skirmish along McPherson's

Ridge. It is well before noon on July 1, 1863, and as I face the battlefield that stretches out before me, I realize that I am now responsible for all Union soldiers upon it. I must focus. There is no room for error.

I ride from McPherson's Ridge to Cemetery Hill and Seminary Ridge. Under my command, all troops in the First Corps acquit themselves well, fighting with daring and mettle. The secesh charge and charge again, but they can make no headway against our troops. What's more, the task of the Union soldiers is nearly impossible, I know this. We are waiting for reinforcements, and as we wait, my troops fight on, though they are heavily outnumbered.

I see a place where a change in strategy must be implemented. I order a rear-guard action and note with satisfaction that my troops follow my orders briskly to move to the heights that surround Gettysburg. This will put us in the best positions to both attack and defend. These strategic movements will also give our own troops more time to establish ground on the perimeter of the battlefield. This way, they will be better able to defend against advancing secesh.

I moved constantly throughout the day, leading 9,500 men in brutal combat. I ordered position changes and even repelled an attack by secesh that came at us from two different directions. It was as exhilarating as it was terrifying, for I will not say that combat of all kinds evokes terror in the heart of a reasonable man. After 5 hours, we could no longer hold out, and the rebels broke into our defensive line. We were pushed back, but we were not beaten. I am proud of my men. I also admit to a bit of pride in myself. My wife Mary will be proud, too, when I write to her of today's events.

> **ANALYZE THIS**
> Compare Doubleday's experience of the war to General Lee's. How are the perspectives similar? How are they different?

Major General Abner Doubleday and his wife Mary were strong supporters of President Abraham Lincoln.

The First Corps, who fought alone for much of this first day before reinforcements arrived, will receive a special commendation in my report on today's activities. They certainly deserve immense credit. I do hope that General Meade will be pleased with my efforts as well. Naturally, I am well trained

THE BATTLE OF ANTIETAM IS THE DEADLIEST ONE-DAY BATTLE IN ALL OF AMERICAN MILITARY HISTORY.

and prepared for such responsibility. I attended the United States Military Academy at West Point, and fought in the Mexican-American War. I even acquitted myself well, if I do say so myself, in the early battles of this Civil War—at the Second Battle of Bull Run and the Battle of Antietam.

In fact, a thing of which I am most proud is that I, as second-in-command at Fort Sumter, ordered the first line of shots fired upon secessionist forces intent on taking over the federal fort. Thus, it could be said that I am the one to begin this war. I certainly aim to finish it as successfully as I started. So you see? I am certainly no stranger to the battlefield, but this level of fighting calls for a level of fast thinking and brute force that I was afraid I could not manage. I am happy to say that my performance, as well as that of my men, saved the day today, on this first day of the

THINK ABOUT IT
Determine the main point of this chapter and pick out two pieces of evidence that support it.

campaign. General Meade will not fail to notice this, I am sure of it.

It is July 2, 1863, day two of this horrid campaign. On the first day we suffered casualties and deaths too great to count, and yet I ended the day indulging in hubris. I let my pride cloud my focus and lost sight of what is most important. There are men who fought more bravely and who gave their lives to this great cause. This I must keep this in mind.

Oh! But it is hard. It is hard because I have been stung by humiliation and betrayal by men I trusted. Men I counted among my friends. I know what some of them think of me. I know they think I am pompous and overbearing, but that is just my way. I accept others for their faults, and I had felt secure that mine were tolerated as well. I was wrong.

General Oliver O. Howard submitted a report to General Winfield Scott Hancock about the events on the first day of fighting. General Hancock brought this

General George Meade was criticized for his decision to not pursue General Lee and the Confederates at the Battle of Gettysburg. He won a decisive victory for the Union, but he lost the chance to end the war.

report to Meade. Though the report contained false information about me, Meade believed it. General Howard said that it was my fault that the Union line of defense gave way late in the evening. Now I have been replaced by John Newton, an old friend and West Point classmate of mine, but a far less experienced

THE GETTYSBURG ADDRESS

President Lincoln came to Gettysburg to dedicate a cemetery for soldiers from both sides. Edward Everett, a well-known speaker, talked for 2 hours, and then Lincoln spoke. He spoke for about 2 minutes and said 272 words. Yet, those words of the Gettysburg Address are some of the most famous in U.S. history.

officer. Though I formally requested to be reinstated to my former position of authority, Meade has turned me down. I can barely stand the shame! And yet I must not lose sight of our important work. If I am to be demoted, so be it. I will do my best no matter what.

On day three, Meade placed me in charge of the Vermont brigade. Under my orders, they flanked and shut down Confederate forces. Some secesh had already reached Union lines and tried to take Union guns, but the Vermont boys fought furiously and beat them back. The rebels called their attack "Pickett's Charge." Well, it was my Vermont boys who clutched their near-victory away and sent them howling in retreat. I know I sound pompous and self-absorbed as I regale this story, but if I don't tell it like it is, I have learned from experience that no one will.

I can take not receiving credit or accolades for my own achievements in battle, but I will not have my soldiers overlooked. It simply is not right.

On July 4, 1863, when the Battle of Gettysburg was finally over, Elisha Hunt Rhodes of the Second Rhode Island Volunteer Infantry noted the relief. He wrote, "Was ever the Nation's birthday celebrated in such a way before?"

It seems we have come to the end of the Gettysburg campaign. The Confederate Army is in full retreat. I believe we will not see them again soon on northern soil. They were fools to try to move the fight north of the Mason-Dixon Line. From here on out, the burden of warfare will be theirs to bear. After all, they are the ones who are in the wrong.

TIMELINE
The Battle of Gettysburg

A Confederate infantry brigade spots Union cavalry on the way to Gettysburg.

TUESDAY, JUNE 30

The battle begins. Both Confederate and Union soldiers descend on the small farming town of Gettysburg. In all, there are 90,000 troops from both sides. The skirmishing continues until nightfall.

WEDNESDAY, JULY 1

Union General George Meade arrives. Confederate General Robert E. Lee orders two of his generals to attack Union forces, but one delays. Many feel this gives the Union soldiers time to regroup and fortify their defensive lines.

THURSDAY, JULY 2

FRIDAY,
JULY 3

General George Pickett commands 15,000 Confederate troops to charge up Cemetery Ridge. Union artillery devastates the "Pickett's Charge." Lee orders the Confederate Army to retreat.

SATURDAY,
JULY 4

The Confederate Army begins a full retreat to Virginia.

NOVEMBER 19,
1863

A section of the Gettysburg battlefield is dedicated as a cemetery and final resting place for fallen Union soldiers. Abraham Lincoln gives the Gettysburg Address.

GETTYSBURG ADDRESS

Nearby, Nov. 19, 1863, in dedicating the National Cemetery, Abraham Lincoln gave the address which he had written in Washington and revised after his arrival at Gettysburg the evening of November 18.

45

Look, Look Again

Take a close look at this illustration of the Battle of Gettysburg and answer the following questions:

1. What would a civilian see in this picture? What would a resident of the town where the fighting took place think about having the battle take place so close to where regular people lived?

2. What would the leader of the Confederate soldiers see in this picture? Would the leader believe his soldiers could be successful in this fight? What type of leadership skills would he need to provide for them?

3. What would the leader of the Union soldiers see in this picture? Would the leader believe his soldiers would be successful in this fight? What type of leadership skills would he need to help his soldiers succeed?

GLOSSARY

allies *(AL-lies)* states and countries that formally recognize and cooperate with one another, usually by signing treaty

artillery *(are-TILL-er-ee)* ordnance or large guns used in land warfare

Confederates *(Con-FED-er-etts)* soldiers and others who supported the Confederate States of America, a faction of southern states that wanted to secede from the United States of America during the U.S. Civil War

feisty *(FAI-stee)* spirited, lively, and courageous

fend *(FEND)* to take care of oneself without help from others

grief *(GRREEF)* deep sorrow

invincible *(in-VIN-sih-bul)* unbeatable

morale *(mor-AL)* a sense of confidence and high spirits

pathetic *(puh-THET-ick)* sadness that causes others to feel pity

setback *(SET-bak)* a mishap that causes progress to reverse

Union *(YOON-yun)* the northern states that opposed the seceding Confederate states in the South during the U.S. Civil War.

LEARN MORE

FURTHER READING

Alleman, Tillie Pierce. *At Gettysburg: Or What a Girl Saw and Heard of the Battle.* London: Forgotten Books, 2018.

Randolph, Jennifer, ed. *Civil War and Reconstruction: Rebellion and Rebuilding.* New York: PowerKids Press, 2018.

Wright, John D. *50 Things You Should Know About the Civil War.* London: QEB Publishing, 2017.

WEBSITES

The Battle of Gettysburg
https://www.civilwar.org/learn/civil-war/battles/battle-gettysburg-facts-summary
This website describes what happened during the Battle of Gettysburg.

Historic Site
https://www.nps.gov/gett/index.htm
This website explains the battle and will help you plan a visit to the historic site where the Battle of Gettysburg took place.

INDEX

Army of the Potomac, 18, 21
artillery, 9, 11, 30, 31, 45

Battle of Antietam, 36, 37
Battle of Chancellorsville, 18, 19, 24

Cemetery Hill, 24, 25, 33
Confederate, 9, 13, 15, 18, 19, 28, 30, 31, 39, 41, 43, 44, 45, 46

Gettysburg Address, 40, 45

Lincoln, President Abraham, 19, 23, 35, 40, 45

Meade, Major General George Gordon, 19, 20, 21, 23, 36, 38, 39, 40, 41, 44

Pickett, George, 23, 29, 30, 31, 41, 45

Union, 5, 6, 10, 13, 15, 17, 24, 25, 26, 27, 28, 30, 31, 32, 33, 39, 40, 41, 44, 45, 46
United States Military Academy at West Point, 20, 37, 40

ABOUT THE AUTHOR

Kristin J. Russo is a university English lecturer. She loves teaching, reading, writing, and learning new things. She and her husband live near Providence, Rhode Island, in a small house surrounded by flower gardens. They have three grown children and three rescue dogs.